Let Us Be Raucous

Also by Lynne Handy

IN THE TIME OF PEACOCKS
SPY CAR AND OTHER POEMS
THE UNTOLD STORY OF EDWINA
WHERE THE RIVER RUNS DEEP

Let Us Be Raucous

Authored and Illustrated by Lynne Handy

Push On Press

Let Us Be Raucous, Copyright ©2018 Lynne Handy

http://lynnehandy.com/

All rights reserved. No part of this book may be reproduced, scanned or distributed in any printed or electronic form without permission.

This is a work of fiction. Names, characters, businesses, places, events and incidents are either the products of the author's imagination or used in a fictitious manner. Any resemblance to actual persons, living or dead, or actual events is purely coincidental.

Published by Push On Press

ISBN: 978-0692119402

Dedicated to the memory of my brother, Carl Francis Handy

Acknowledgments

Thanks to Gloria Boyer for editing the poems and short stories in this collection.

Thanks also to Kevin Moriarity for formatting the book and designing a cover for my raucous girl.

Revolution is the festival of the oppressed.
Germaine Greer

Have you not made a universal shout,
That the Tiber trembled underneath her banks
To hear the replication of your sounds
Made in her concave shores?

William Shakespeare. *Julius Caesar*, Act I

Contents

- Poems 1
  - Let Us Be Raucous 2
  - Country Road 4
  - Visiting Aunt Sadie 5
  - Grasshopper Summer 6
  - Now I Am Become Death 8
  - Pink Oblivion 9
  - Two Years Before the Pill 12
  - Grafitti 13
  - My Guernica 15
  - Worm in the Bud 17
  - Door 20
  - I Am 22
  - Battle 23
  - Swash and Muzzle 25
  - Testimony 27
  - Bridled 29
  - Memo 31
  - Forget-Me-Nots 33
  - Little Elephant 35
  - Storm on the River 36

Not Harry Lime's Dots 37
Mother Goose for Militant Children 40
Prediction 42
White Star 44
Purification (A Found Poem) 46
Twenty-Four Lines for the Wordman 50
Wilson Street Café 52
Dandelion Danse 54
Flowering Tea 55
Poet's Heart 58
Escaping the Tomb 60
Mind Dance 61
Winter of Self Love 63
Memories of Clan 66
Folk 67
DNA 68
Red Lilies 69
Woman at Skara Brae 71
Grandmother 73
King Puck 76
Ode to a Kerry Cow 78
Sacred Isle 80
The Ferry Fly 82

Gathering the Mistletoe	84
Short Stories	85
Dina, Warrior Child	86
Walls	90
Me Too	96

Poems

Let Us Be Raucous
--From Disturbed's *The Sound of Silence*

The singer asks, *Where is our courage?*
It's there in his face, the rings in his chin.
in his voice, journeyman pure
with rock titan rasp that brazens the words
of the truth-teller poet. It's in the way
the hazan calls out the word *whisper*.
It's in we who need saving from folly.
It's in Isaiah 42: 20. Observe; hear.
It's in me. Give me my pen.

Let Us Be Raucous

Country Road

A road angles past our nested farm.
Silt treads and grassy strip support at midpoint
railroad ties where locomotives chug at dusk,
whistles wailing lonesome in the mist.

Hot summer days,
I press my ear against the velvet drift,
hear the thrum of tractors rolling out to fields.
Dust between my toes, I slide a stem of timothy
from its sheath, chew the sugary tip.

Wild onion ripples in the breeze
the day my uncle hefts his gun,
leads Mama's bulldog down that road.
Old and sick, Pooch no longer barks—
he's more trouble than he's worth.

We hear the shot.

Mama cries out, grasps the cast-iron stove.
Eyes wide, I hide behind the cellar door.

Visiting Aunt Sadie

At great-aunt Sadie's house
we sleep in musty rooms
between cool sheets. We
eat bologna sandwiches
and lick chocolate ice cream cones.
We slip our arms into long-ago shirtwaists
and push our feet into demitasse shoes.
We go walking around the village at twilight,
and help neighbors weed marigold patches.
We pick cherries from the trees,
drop them into buckets like gold.
We climb out on the two-story roof
to better see the stars.
Auntie is sympathetic to our dreams.

Grasshopper Summer

My twelfth summer,
heat came in unremitting waves.
Leaves hissed in spitless breezes,
lilacs languished on their stems.
In a side-yard plot, carrots rooted
into rot, corn shriveled
in cemetery fields, grasshoppers
ate holes in the sullen wash
we pinned to a clothesline rope.
Everyone went partially mad.

I slew the grasshoppers.
It was my passion and my plan.
Under the pitiless sun, enrapt,
as tears streaked down my cheeks,
I drowned them in a galvanized tub
filled with tepid water from the creek.
Their corpses floated like wafer-thin goodbyes.
I hanged them from a clothespin gallows,
their wings folded in farewell.
I built a guillotine of razor and wood,
slammed down the blade,
blew kisses to their sliced-off heads.
Mama and Daddy said not a word.
Grandparents, uncles, aunts walked past
my execution chamber,
smiled, went on their way,
everyone too dried out to talk.

LET US BE RAUCOUS

I got my period that September.
Years later, I understood
the surge within, without,
the grasshoppers
bearing the swelter of my rage.

Now I Am Become Death

(Bhagavad Gita, quoted in a 1945 speech by J. Robert Oppenheimer*)*

Tulips, cranberry pink, petals agape,
pistil sights dead center.

Target: two cities—

Bombers shriek through meshed clouds
on a summer's day:
Hiroshima first,
Nagasaki three days later.

Fat Man and Little Boy are ironic names
for death deliverers, on an airship,
named *Enola* for the pilot's mother—
better *Satan's Hand* or *Devil's Curse*.

A blast splits the sky
with insidious, infinite light;
then comes a never-never cloud,
and atomic waves—
an empire erased.

The world is aftershocked.

Fragile tulips nest among daffodils.
All have glowing centers and cling to the far side
of Ghost Mountain.

Pink Oblivion

During the Red Scare, I ducked my skinny frame
beneath a school desk, and though in a buffered state,
still saved seeds to plant in the aftermath.

Radioactive winds never blew my way.
Nuclear rays have not seared my arms and face,
nor have mutant cells invaded my blood   so far.

But the sickness is jack-screwed through my core.
I birthed its terror to my children who, like me,
are so traumatized they're numb.
We go on living in pink oblivion,
ignoring thoughts that annihilation
is just an itch away.

What else can be done?

Two Years Before the Pill

> Indiana's recent law requires that miscarried
> and aborted fetuses be interred or cremated.
> (*New York Times*, 4/8/2016)

Without warning, my uterus cramped
and the dregs of a coupling drained
between my legs.

That misbegotten mess that spiraled
down the toilet bowl, that necrotic blend
of him and me, I was glad to see it go.

I had three children. Another
before my twenty-second year
would be more than I could bear.

An Indiana senator claims
my little baby lost its life,
and thus requires state protection.
Should I have scooped it
from the drain
to mourn, bury or cremate?

Governor Pence's phone keeps ringing—
Indiana women report the status of their menses.

Grafitti

    To my three daughters

When you told me,
I believed you straightaway.
Truth is a skinny redhead speaking plain.

The day dawned with a bright sun
and suffered a permanent eclipse.
There you stood
in drab green T-shirt and scruffy jeans,
eyes dark, steady.

I acted in a blink, severing him with the quick ink
of a judge's pen. Like a slur your dad
whirred away in his Toyota.

I'd been blinded by my grocery list, sterile floors,
vacuumed rugs, futile hugs. My Presbyterian past
with decent men. All that kept me from
saving my blossoms from their crushing.

If I were to do it over, I'd let the dishes go,
ignore sticky handprints
on the doors, welcome grit-crunch
on the floors. I'd serve hot dogs and chips,
run with you in the sun
and find the nick in time
to save you.

I'd be the friend you needed.
I'd understand
>　why *you* hated your body.
>　　why *you* flaunted yours, built fires, and stole.
>　　why *you* patrolled the yard with Tuffy, the battle cat.

Forty years later, I say to one of you: *Let's spray "pedophile"*
on his tombstone with black paint. You say: *Two old women*
skulking around a graveyard with an empty can of pain.

My Guernica

My grandsons, Gideon and Matthew, killed themselves.
Before Gideon died, he shot his mother, who survived.
Don't these calamities happen to other people?
--from Diary of Lynne Handy, Fort Worth, Texas, February 2006

It's all there on the newsprint.
Painting of agony and war:
A matador, he is dead,
his arm and blade severed near the hilt.
The bull's dagger-tongue goes up in smoke,
a sword gores a horse
whose lips peel to bare mortuary teeth.
The dead-eyed woman
squints at heaven,
a child rigors in her arms.
Bombillas for hope.

The day of the attack, the refrigerator coos
like Heinkel fifty-twos. Bombs are direct hits.
One boy is dead from a gunshot; one jumps off a bridge.
A daughter loses half her jaw to a bullet.
With a lick of their tongues, two women grieve fallen sons.
Teeth roll like pearls on the living room rug,
blood thinned with rain runs red on the porch,
half a brain stains the wall in the corridor,
a detective's white card waits by the phone.

I sensed impending catastrophe.
Strong-minded children test bonds,
but this was more than that—
a wrenching apart, inflexibility,
a craving to blame. I was a quail
with feigned dead wing, dancing
to save her nest. I danced with words,
pleading for peace. I counseled
with priests, therapists.
I prayed on my knees
as unholies do, writhing in pain
on arthritic bones.

A three-eyed nurse says: *Guernica has come.*
Like the matador, my pretty grandsons are dead.
My daughter's baby lips, which compared my breasts
to apples, now propped open like a guppy's.
She will live. The bullet lodges near her left ear.

I sit on a chair and howl.
This is written on newsprint, this telling.

Worm in the Bud

But let concealment, like a worm i'th bud / feed on her damask cheek.
Twelfth Night, William Shakespeare

The invisible worm…has found out thy bed of crimson joy.
The Sick Rose, William Blake

There amid the larkspur, a dimpled rose
clings to thorny stem; petals wimpling,
it grows singly, secretes a crimson joy.

Night breezes fan into the garden,
kiss the rose with deference—
slight, but there. For the larkspur,
they have less appetite.

Under cloud-capped moon,
the scavenger appears from earthen den,
a deadly worm squirms up the stem,
bites the stigma adhering to the rosy ovary,
pulls each silken petal outward to oblivion,
then turns to settle on the riddled bush,
its abettal clear with laws of nature.
The worm has license to destroy—
a tug, a chomp, a devouring,
a devastating plague; the garden gone
unless a green-gloved hand intervenes.

I employ no champion,
no one to snare the worms tearing at my heart,

suppressing kindness, empathy, healthy acts
of loving. No, I'm kept grieving and apart.

Door*

A wreath raked with frost,
a door armed to repel the hoary eye
of winter
        The grit of loss still grinds against
            my softer parts.
          I've thought of dying
Why not? There's the gas oven, like Plath
      I could choose that path or pills like Teasdale
         or Crane's leap in the sea—

Out there a snowed-over hell
in me too, in lieu
of living

March: whitetail deer approach
on horn-tipped hooves,
feed on acorns by the porch

My blood pulses through clots of ice,
    warms—
      I fear leaving myself and
hear
the birds of spring appear and
I am nearer the door. Do I
    design a new self—
        one more inclined to—

but leaving me would grieve me

*Published in *Pegasus*, Kentucky State Poetry Society, Winter/Spring Issue 2015
*Published in *Reverie Fair*, Winter 2016
*Published in *Spy Car and other Poems*, Lynne Handy, Push On Press, 2015

I Am

a cake in a holy pan,
a child who saw through walls,
a wife, scoffing at breakfast,
a mother duck,
      who watched hawks take her young,
a rescuer of floppy-eared mutts with black coats,
a lover of beets, carrots, parsnips,
and all things rooted in soil,
a wailing witness to suicides, estrangements, and hard partings,
a branch in rough waters,
a wolf bitch howling at southern skies,
a flight risk,
a white light that never quite went out,
a grandmother clock moving forward,
a stroker of velvets,
a gnawer of chocolate,
a finder of words like *Vantablack* and *thruple*,
a jotter of taut phrases,
a flame of kept memories,
a chirper of wind songs,
a cheer-leader for truth,
and a conundrum. I have
three-eyes—one to see backward.
I am Athena, the judge,
and Venus, goddess of erotic dawns,
I thirst for water and sleep
and look to the stars for relief.

Battle

Hard to set my grip protect my mind with a hard hat
and flex my sex with sense and not surrender. Still he slides
into the pool of me and for a while I'm on a cattail ride
I see which way that's leading,
and set off to join the mob of angry mamas
and claim the right of way,
passing off on peas, the shell-outs and sell-outs,
and de Pizan's ghost, her allegory of empty hopes for widows,
'cause I want to warn my captive sex—the war wears on
and temptations pouf my sumptuous body like dandelions
and I am deluded by tumid water lilies—
but wrench away and broken wedlocks set me free

from the tyranny Abigail and Mary decried at revolution's dawn.
Hail Seneca Falls and Elizabeth and Susan B and Emily
and forego marriage or marry an acolyte but freely be.
Charlotte paints the yellow doom and Margaret cheers the empty womb.
Yet Still the tempting ache for hard muscled arms—
Surrender is a coward's word, *love*, a madness begun with Eve,
that mewly mere on whom malefactors dumped their fear.

Nice is what I was trained for.
Let me not play nice in this world of rape and incest
and fists demanding dominance and veils and glass ceilings
and forced baby-bearing and six-inch heels and ankle sprains.
Let me not play nice in this world of screwed over salaries

and a lover critical of the length of a skirt and the need
for anti-grope laws in the workplace.

Bella, Germaine, and Gloria rebuked and warned.
Too many women say, "I don't want to sound like a feminist,
but—"
Sound like a feminist! Own yourself! Possession is nine tenths of
the law.
Push on.

And you—you get away from me.
I can't write with your hot breath on my neck.

Swash and Muzzle

I've wondered why I've studied so many male poets, as if women
were too Eve-like, too divine, weak-minded, or insane to write
on great themes of humankind. Of course, there was Sappho;
here and there on cartonnage we find her stanzas, but I can't recite
from memory one line of her verse. Fathers of the early Church,
preferring women mute, besmirched her name, burned her work.

I've wondered why college lit courses
raked me with the phallic take on life, when, indisputably,
there were truths no man could know—
like menstruation, birthing, humility, and compromise—
but yet, the distaff side, its cleft of wool unspun, had no outflow
of thought because prideful, shag-maned leos held sway,
forcing females to wait centuries to have their say.

In century fifteen, Christine di Pisan, writer of books and poems,
was vexed for her sex (widows especially) and assailed *Roman
de la Rose*, a popular lay, that portrayed women as lustful and cheap.
Mixing self-deprecation with reason and rage, she civilized France.
This laudable mother of sensible mien approached men aslant,
not head on, like modern mothers who are less tolerant.

Harold Bloom, lit-lion decider, feared the taint of outsider voices,
so compiled his canon of great writers (men: twenty-two;
women: four) and bounced them high on Olympian clouds.
There clustered lit-lustered wonderful men whose purview
defined fit emotion and extolled the most noble goal: war.
Men only—sufficiently gifted to lift the sword of metaphor.

From his house of gables, Hawthorne bewailed that "damned mob
of scribbling women" when their successes affected his sales.
Wordsworth reputedly revived the English sonnet: not so—
it was Charlotte Smith. Those Romantic rhymers scorned females.
With upturned noses, they termed lady-verse
"the middle order of poesy." Women's minds:
"a Sargasso Sea"—this from Pound, a rabid fan of Mussolini.

I sigh, wondering if in men's measure, the *feminine sphere*
contains a brain or is *sphere* a metaphor for moon, ovum, or breast?
I've wondered if there is a masculine sphere, but probably not—
it has the wrong shape. What's kingly about a globe? Best
look to a skyscraper, rocket ship, torpedo, pine tree, piece of chalk,
ray-finned gar, Cuban cigar, party hat, or asparagus stalk.

Testimony

I smell it—
testosterone bones the very air I breathe,
raping seas and waterways, regulating wombs
and ovaries, paring healthcare to a nub.
I smell it in warlords' jizzy elbow-rubs,
in stilled dissent and parody;
in decay of human brain cells,
contempt for learning. It is strongest
in the threat of nuclear cinders
and human ash, and truths hidden
in the swamp-clot of lies.

This frazzled world needs correction.
'Til yesterday, we were progressing,
but then a curtain dropped
on science, sanity, and good sense.

It's time to sanitize,
revitalize the world.
Infuse it with truth,
train youth in humanitarian pursuits,
gather all the terrible bombs,
sink them into a sea-safe,
and melt the key; revere the oceans,
heat the world with only sun,
respect the intellect of women,
read the beatitudes, a really good primer

for the lost. Erect monuments to poets,
inscribe their words in the sky.

Let calm breezes waft
in tropes of humility and good will;
a butterfly propulsion,
a timbre of fragile wings
made momentous by their mission
to save the world from testosterone.

Published in *Writers Resist*, Issue 55:08, February, 2018

Bridled

-from "11 Years Old, a Mom, and Pushed to Marry Her Rapist in Florida"
Nicholas Kristoff, *New York Times*, May 26, 2017

She's eleven,
loves God, Ariana Grande,
chocolate candy, school, the Golden rule.
She's destined to teach or pen anthems to Jesus.

Scene unseen: God's basement. Blinds
squint at the creep of night. Walled
hippos climb aboard the gopher wood ark.
Hot breath sears her neck.
Belt unbuckled panties tear cries drowned out
while upstairs
members say the Creed.

She wants a Huffy Cruiser bike--
not a baby—not a man,
but his seed like a weed
takes root in her womb.

Wedding day,
she wakes up whiney.
Bridled in an eyelet dress,
she pokes her toes in Mary Janes.
Mama styles her curls just so,
adds glow

to palish cheeks and chin.
Toting lilies from Granny's garden,
she truckles to the altar,
Lamb-like, feeling the spikes.

In Deuteronomy,
sages demanded rapists wed their victims.
That's after the part
where Lot offered his daughters to a mob,
and before Judges, where the Levite
tossed his concubine to the rabble,
then sliced her savaged body into twelfths,
sending them off as proof of low morality.
Selah. (Maybe means *forever*.)

In twenty-seven states, desert law prevails. Selah.
In the sweet by and by, sings the choir, we *will meet
on that beautiful shore*. She has traded education
for procreation, will learn to swaddle babies,
coddle eggs, sweep the floor, adore Jesus,
find ways not to cry *in the sweet by and by*.

Memo

To the buckled buckaroos in Washington;
to our bumbling resident prez, to the North Korean pistachio
and Russia's nippled centaur; to jihadi bombers for Allah,
Chinese island-riggers, and jewel-toed sheiks;
to alpha-males everywhere:

I'm sick of living in the clench of male prerogative.
I despise war strut, bombs, and guns; roughshod
rides over truth, morality, fairness, science and good sense.
I hate the stench of low-lying skies, sullied rivers and highways.
What will be left for our children?

Bleeding ovaries! Look to the ages.
Right after she wrenched the universe from her mind,
Gaia gave birth to woman. She then hewed mountains
from molecules, carved out crystalline rivers and seas,
fashioned roses from the folds in her labia, deer from her sinews,
and man from the small bones in her left foot.

You gained the upper hand when a plummeting planet
struck Gaia and laid her out for eons. You wrote
the so-called holy books, gave us church fathers
like Paul and Augustine who took away our power.
You bound our feet and chained our private parts
and bred us so young we died.
You stole our choices, silenced our voices.
You burned us at the stake.

Face up. You've failed and you need to move over.
We are life-givers with a potent type of sanity
based on intuition and good sense. We have compassion;
we care for people, no matter how they look and are.
We deplore death machines as the antithesis of life.
Long ago, we lost our egos in poopy diapers and sweeping floors.
We greet the world with hope because we push newborns
from our wombs. We respect the clarity of sea and sky,
birds in flight, puppies' breath, bare feet, and a lover's kiss.
Women are the most unused resource on planet earth.
We are the solution. Take our hands.

Forget-Me-Nots

Ants ate the dead fly.
They orbited its corpse,
tore it apart
with bear-trap teeth
and bore it away.
Nothing left on the deck—
no wing tip,
not even a stain.

On my way to Dallas,
a dead man passed
in a black hearse
flying a red flag.
A priest drove behind
to tie up loose ends,
his white collar bright
in the sun.

Lunching out,
I read of a man
who overdosed.
At his memorial,
close friends *mea culpa'd*.
No circle of closure,
only wreaths of thyme
and forget-me-nots.

I search the café wall
for something—
reassurance?
Knotholes reveal
a tulip, an erect penis,
a laughing cat,
a maiden's profile
with parted lips.

Little Elephant*

Like Lenin, he lies under glass
but not alone—husked from his own tusk,
he is jammed in the display case with other ivories,
an eland with slender horns, a towering pharaoh,
a finely carved rhino. See how he prances
like a savannah prince, his trunk curling
to reach bananas from a gnarly tree.
His tail lies tight against his backside;
his black eyes—

The sign reads sixty percent off. I long to buy him,
give him a home on my antique desk where my loving hand
can warm his hide, and I can speak to him of my sorrow—
he'd been slain for his tusks, hauled off from his edenic home
to a Chinese factory where an artist scraped and shaped him
into his tiny likeness—but I can't; that would mean
I supported his slaughter, and I'd be like the clerk,
an old woman with Cleopatra eyes who pulls back her dyed hair
to show me flower earrings:
"See," she says," they're made of ivory."

*Published in *Pegasus*, Kentucky State Library Society,
Winter/Spring Issue, 2016

Storm on the River

The river snakes a pathway
through the valley.
Petrified trees chant a black mass.
Roots part like dragon's lips
to sip the wine, and unruly eddies
snatch driftwood wafers hurtling by.
On the second *kyrie*, an egret genuflects,
lifts its beak to stab a defrocked badger's toe.
Owls hoot blasphemies. We cover our ears.
River winds howl at the pale moon
as we gather the drowning into our catamaran.

Not Harry Lime's Dots
    Inspired by Orlando and the film, *The Third Man*.

Camera: Angled shot of war-torn Vienna.
Zither music, frenzied, pulsing.

From a Viennese Ferris wheel, Harry Lime
glances down at people on the street,
        calls them *dots*.

Close up. You know Harry—the guy
who waters down penicillin
for sick children and makes a killing.
So innocents die. He feels no pity
for the death of dots.
Says so right from between his lips.

Greed and distance
shield him from the dying; he's deaf
to smothered cries for Mama.
He does not comfort the bereaved
or visit graves to lay sprays
of baby's breath and balm.
A dark figure shadowed by slow-
grinding spokes, Harry smiles.
Evil oozes from his skin.

How many bloodfests ago
were innocents massacred in Charleston,
San Bernardino,

Aurora,
Fort Hood,
Sandy Hook,
other schools…?
Will this movie never end?

Tilted bar scene. Orlando.
Nearly one hundred not-dots gunned down here.
Vanishing point beyond the frame.

Mother Goose for Militant Children

    -With help from "Who Killed Cock Robin," "Mary, Mary, Quite Contrary," "There was a Little Man," "I Do Not Like Thee, Dr. Fell," "Wee Willie Winkie," and "Boys and Girls Come Out to Play"

Who killed Cock Robin? Who saw him die?
For my kids,
a mind-freezing find—
that photo in *Jet* magazine.
A teen-aged Chicago boy murdered and mutilated,
laid out on white satin for the nation to grieve.
His killers went free,
lived to boast of their crime in *Look* magazine.

With silver bells and cockle shells,
and pretty maids all in a row
(pet names for torture devices).
I lined up my kids in front of the TV
to bear witness to humanity screaming
as Mississippi police
set dogs on protestors
assembled in peace,
blasted them with hoses,
smashed their skulls with clubs.

There was a little man, and he had a little gun...
When a shooter killed
a black messiah
on a Memphis balcony,

Let Us Be Raucous

I cried, held my kids tight.
He was our leader too.

I do not like thee, Dr. Fell. The reason why—I cannot tell.
Old fears breed open season on black men—
they're shot down on the streets.
My kids ask, *Why bullets, not tasers?*
Why shoot to kill?
Aren't there better ways?

Are the children in their beds? For it's now eight o'clock.
My kids live safe in their neighborhood.
On Chicago's South Side,
gangs, up to no good,
shoot kids at play
on porches, at family barbecues.

Boys and girls, come out to play. The moon is shining, bright as day.
Come with a whoop, come with a call. Come with a good will or not at all.

Prediction

> *Curses are like young chickens, they always come home to roost.*
> Robert Southey, "The Curse of Kehama"

*The chickens
are coming home
to roost,*
warned
Malcolm X,
implying
JFK's death
was karma
for the black deeds
of white men.

Barred Rocks,
black-and-white
feathered,
tethered
on little claw feet
like Sandburg's fog,
flock
innocuously.

Leghorns
peck away
under
black men
dangling
from trees.

Let Us Be Raucous

Wyandotte Reds
circled in mesh
peck away
as bodies clot
city streets.

Chanticleers
peck away
as hate spreads
from Georgia's
red clay,
right up
Highway 35
to St. Paul
and all the way down
to Dallas
and Baton Rouge.

Where is home when night falls?
Where will the chickens roost?

White Star

Flagging star,
white, symbol of purity,
shadows all Texans
in a false flap
of freedom,

flies proud over Dallas,
a city built on old lizard bones
buried in lava laps,
now gleaming,
flush with greenbacks
and home of the sushi burrito.

Flies over fiefdoms
and sleek aquamarine pools
with fire-bowl torches
and moated driveways,

but the past hemorrhages
not-so-long-ago Jim Crow.
*Don't touch your lips
to white fountains! Don't sit
on my toilet seat! Don't look
at white women!* Sadly
the white star

Let Us Be Raucous

drapes over South Dallas poor
where police shoot
when they go through the door.

Flies at half-staff for five brave men in blue
shot at a peaceful rally. Police sent a robot
to blast the shooter clean off the news.

I stare at the flag,
what noble hues--
brave red, true blue,
the purest white star.
How— and when—will someone win
this endless civil war?

Purification (A Found Poem)

(Timothy Hornyak, "Trial by Meltdown," *Science*, 4 March 2016)
("Misogi Shuho," Tsubaki Grand Shrine of America)
(Reuters, "The Robots Sent Into Fukushima have Died," *Newsweek*, 9 March 2016)

At Fukushima, robots are critical players in the cleanup.
Some float or swim through pools formed in the bowels of
buildings, crawl through pipes, cut and remove debris.

Izanagi-no-OKami conducted the first Misogi-Shuho
purification rite following his visit to the Yomi (world of death)

Quince, the first Japanese bot to enter the wrecked buildings,
gathers data for radiation maps, samples airborne radioactive
particles, and monitors radiation dose rates.

Izanagi's purpose was to wash away defilement, cleanse his body
from pollutants

Toshiba's quadruped inspection robot has greater mobility
over crawling robots. This robot verifies there were no leaks in the
crucible holding the partially melted-down reactor.

Prior to entering the Tachibana River to cleanse completely,
Izanagi rids himself of all his possessions

Let Us Be Raucous

ASTACO-SoRa, a shovel-wielding robot, has done yeoman's work removing debris—sheet metal, fallen ducts, and concrete chunks. It has swappable grippers and blades.

Raccoon is a nuclear-hardened maid that scrubs floors. Its decontamination work has helped tamp down radiation levels.

> *Finding a spot in the river not too swift and not too slow, Izanagi enters the river to purify himself. Many Kami are created from this act, Kami of wrong-doing, as well as Kami to rectify wrong-doing*

> *Through the sacred technology of Misogi Shuho you can feel OKami of Great Nature as your direct parent and receive divine guidance and love*

Epitaph

Radiation destroyed
the robots' wiring,
rendering them useless

Forget me not
twanged the noble bots
whose mission fizzled
as their wiring sizzled

Twenty-Four Lines for the Wordman*
for Frank Rutledge

Burning wordman,
riverside rhythm-maker,
closes one eye with the night
but keeps the other aslant
so he'll not miss
the glint of daybreak.

With gentleman's grace,
he lifts his fork, matches
anklebones as he sits,
weighs his sugar intake—
Is a cookie allowed? One,
only one, if you please.

Barricaded in a corner,
he grins as others charade,
offers wry observations—
unveils a firefly soul.
Try to capture him,
he's gone—ahead of us.

Taking the stage with slow feet,
he feels the upthrust
of crowds, shapeshifts
into performer extraordinaire.
Watch the poet's wind-up.
He pitches his verse.

LET US BE RAUCOUS

*Published in *Pegasus*, Kentucky State Poetry Society, Summer/August, 2016.

Wilson Street Café

Peapod room, coffee
fragrant— arabica, Kona, Jamaican blue;
twenty-two types of tea,
        including oolong, chai, and chamomile.

Tiny tables, vagrant chairs,
back door for hippies, jet-set
treks in through the front.

A window view of passing cars,
the sobbing river sky, thin birches,
        and old brick shops with New Age merch.

Amateur art on walls—
how many kinds of owls can there be?

Sweat-slicked joggers
lean on the counter for lattes.

Guitar man growls
"Help Me Make It Through the Night,"
though it is day.

Waitress whisks buttered scones
to a gab of matrons in tights.

Hemingway twin composes in repose.

Guru passes through
        with studied simper
        on his long face.

Customers tote laptops, pens,
notebooks, wait for sparks.
Ideas sting like riled wasps.

Let Us Be Raucous

Scrunched like revolutionaries,
       recluse poets crunch them
       with their teeth,
       spit out the wings,
smash the febrile bodies into verse.

Dandelion Danse

Something astral about dandelions--
their golden faces twinkling
on the morning green.
Generous of heart, they spread love
to rich and poor alike. At spring's onset,
stems leap *en pointe* to receive the sun,
and sawtooth leaves unfurl,
extending
their reach with purpose and good will.

It's nature's plan for blooms to live their span,
then turn to seed puffs, scatter in the wind,
but in an act of interruptus,
man, preferring sweeps of grass
with no starry disruption,
lops them with spinning blades,
and soaks their enzymes with herbicides.
The former results in beheaded stems,
flailing *en l'air*—
truly, a danse macabre—
and the latter, death by herbicide,
presents grotesqueries
of writhing pipes *a terre*.

Here lies nature, once wild and free,
now savaged by conformity.

Flowering Tea

Ladies from the poet's society went to tea
at the old Tickington Inn in the tin-roofed room
where poets and sages had gathered in another age.
A violin moaned. Anna sat by her mother; a blue ribbon
tied up her tow-headed curls and matched her pretty lace
dress. From the west window streamed sprinkles of dust.

Anna smothered a sneeze. *Drat that dust!*
complained Mother. *It's sifted into our tea!*
But Anna saw in the drift-fall, not dust, but lace,
a lace-gowned woman descending into the room,
reading verse, yes, descending on a ribbon
of words, "thees and thous," from another age.

The woman of lace seemed of indeterminate age.
She was slim; her hair, the color of dust.
In her upsweep, not a single gay ribbon.
Plain, she was; her eyes a shade of over-brewed tea.
She slipped down into the chattering room
in a gown of silvery, shimmery lace.

Anna leaped up from the table to lace
her small hand in the poet's. She was of an age
to trust, to find wonder; so there in the room
where others saw shafts of pulsating dust,
Anna welcomed an inscrutable poet, led her to tea,
poured a demitasse cup, and cut her a ribbon

of cinnamon cake and another thin ribbon
of tart and offered a thimble of whiskey to lace
the tiny demitasse cup of Flowering tea.
Her elders laced theirs (she was of an age
to notice): her mind was not clouded with dust.
She was soberest female in the tin-roofed room.

Envision that old cherrywood, chandeliered room:
a gypsy tune, ladies sipping and tipsy—a ribbon
of rhyme, cadenced and clear, heard aloft in the dust-
rimmed room and a girl's quivering form draped in lace--
Anna was twelve and a half, a sweet primrosy age
for wonder and more, that day at the lady poets' tea.

Anna remembers the poet, the room, the Flowering tea.
Now in her ninetieth year of life—
memories unfurl and swirl on ribbons of dust and lace.

Poet's Heart

I'm a poet, I say,
watching my heart pulsate
on the computer screen.
The technologist smiles,
keeps his eyes on the monitor,
then rattles off a few lines
rife with rhyme; I tell him end-rhyme
is passe, that he must compose
in conversational cadences. He grins.

I am quiet, watching my blood flow,
imaged in bright red, royal blue—
and when it gushes, yellow.
Doppler effect. Beat on.

*Do you know what part
was damaged by your heart attack?*

The back, I reply.
I see the bubble in the wall.
Report will read: *akinetic.*

Beat on, brave muscle.
My personal pump.
You and I know of recouping loss.
We've fielded erotic entanglement,
sorrow for our suicides, gratitude
for a strawberry-covered cake,

Let Us Be Raucous

hopeless estrangements,
rage at the world's horrors,
starbursts of love for the youth at my table
and translated it all into verse.

Beat on.

Escaping the Tomb

The audiologist tuned my hearing aids full bore today.
I walked my little dog, heard her tags clinking in the dawn,
heard hijacked lilacs lick the wind, the swish of jaunty leaves.
Found my way to a posh cafe, had ahi tuna and cashews,
listened to a hash of conversation, heard a tune,
the thrum of drums, the mnemonic nosh of bells.
When I left, a woman said, "Such a lovely lady,"
as I held open an elevator door.
With those words, she pried chunks from my confinement.
Here was Mary come to lead me from the tomb.

Mind Dance

--You must have chaos within you to give birth to a dancing star.
Friedrich Nietzsche

How goes the dry eye tonight,
the spine that bent to the river wash,
the aching arms that carried dithyrambs
up the mountain slope?
Legs like pegs, feet shambled from skipping,
toe-tipping, gripping stones.
What about the arthritic thumbs,
the sluggish bowel, creaking knees,
the headache following airy spaces,
the iliac artery stenosed at sixty percent,
the body that lies under a quilt, absent of strength?

    Doesn't mean
        I can't dance,
  because the ankle pulses thrive.
  and the mind is jived
        with drum beats, mania,
        and sweet mama juice.

Loose the guitar, swoon that bassoon.
The girl in red sequins
needs no mike to sing blue.
I hump my back like the Gateway Arch.
Nietzche, you devil, I'm an ubermensch,
a super imperative salience going haywire
at the drop of the moon, where I lie unasleep.
Move that triceps brachii—sounds like a Roman god.
Flex neck, fold in shoulders, raise knees,
do the chicken walk. Make like Mick do.
Hips grind those coffee beans   flying free now.
Pirouette, leap like Mischa, the flying femur.
pose like Rudi a man with consummate grace.
Tap like Fred, glide like Ginger, I've a hunger in my belly

for Kelly and Cyd. Moonwalker Mike is switchblade quick.
Let me get down low on my heel and toe.
I'm break dancing, river dancing, tossing in a flamenco.

My neurons are screaming I'm so out of breath.

    But I danced.

Winter of Self Love

Always someone's something—
mommy or honey or...
One day, I asked, *Who am I*
and signed my name in blood so I wouldn't forget.

My children rode off on spavined horses.
My husband landed on his expiration date.
My parents, on theirs. That tether gone,
my siblings created their own lives, apart,
as did I.

In this winter of self-love,
I sled through a spatter of stars,
touch the icy moon with my tongue,
shriek like a newborn,
and shiver the fire of finally being me.

Memories of Clan

When the sun broke through ice-glazed panes,
bestowing light we needed to see:
we were good angels, all of us.
Laughter pealed,
resounded against the creamy walls,
soaked floribunda carpets,
tamped down pains of discontent
and caused us to wonder again at each other.
Roasted meats, potatoes, gravy,
Mother's butterscotch pie graced our table.
Grandma's Blue Willow china,
set on white linen, lent elegance
to the drab order of our lives.
We were stars, we were champions,
we blended into the cosmos of clan.

Oh, magic time!

Folk

Second sons chancing seas for opportunity,
risk-takers, feisty folk with untamed locks,
carved cheekbones, beanpole legs,
their eyes on the horizon.
I am they.

In my left leg lives an Irish jig,
my biceps tighten for a saber strike.
I burn for gypsy tambourines,
crave warm caves and cinnamon tarts,
take the Bible with a crock of salt
and steal its myths for poems.
I flirt with sin—
but wear conscience like a cinder block.

A high-bred grandmother offered grace.
I gripped it tight, my fingers bled.
Celts backhanded me with mystic sight.
I wept for the world's deceit.

Now I see not far from the grave
and bend but never bow. Pride,
fear of extinction, keep me upright.

A priest serves communion
and locks me with his eyes
I am here, I telepath,
What more can one possibly want?

DNA

My DNA streams from the dawn of time.
I dined on couches with Calpurnia
and worshipped at Zeus's shrine.
I huddled in a bog with Og
and with the vestigial horn of my little toe,
dug for seashore clams.

Vanished kings of Euro-kingdoms,
bony brides who died a-birthing,
warriors rigored into crucifixes,
zealots refusing to kiss a pope's ring—
I spring from sturdy folk
who kept steady eyes on freedom's prize.

Red Lilies

An elegy for Thomas Poyner Handy*

Standing tall
on palls of clover,
he musters in at Kankakee,
    sleeves
        his wings in Union blue,
    and flaps off to war.

    Perhaps he hears
    a mystic chord,
    the drums' aortic beat,
    a bugle tucket tinning.

September:
the army camps on columbines
and tramps on river bracken,
ripped by boots and wheels and mules.

Winter gloms in snow and scum. How far away is home?

    Gunshots *hiss* a man afire. Did you see that!
Pop! Pop pop pop. Cannonball and musket fire,
cavalry beats back Company E—
    bayonets smear with blood—
slicked poppies grow in willowed *cricks*.
    Mind those spikes, last cries,
        the ghosts that rise in smoke,

                    fair boys to bones minds cracked.
      Lie low among the spiderwort.

Aim at those gray boys, cousins some.
        Whose blood waters the battlefields?

      Yet, comes reveille,
      red lilies trumpet from the clouds.

God loves him:
young eagle of war,
who never got to fight,
but died of measles on the Ohio shore:
now a photographed sad spirit
that a great-great niece will mourn
and tell goodnight and tuck into a poem.

*Published in *Clementine Unbound*, September, 2016

Woman at Skara Brae
for Dorine Bowman Handy

Archaeologists date the village, discovered in the Orkneys, to around 3100 BC.
("Before Stonehenge," National Geographic, August 2014)

See my mother's ancestress on the ness;
she is that short woman of sturdy build,
speaking to the sky before it pitches black.

She holds a bone she's been puzzling over--
somehow there's a way to shape it to a tool
for scraping silver discs from fish.

With woman's wit, she oversees construction
of her house, setting walls thick
to soften the sea roar,
laying a stone hearth for warmth,
carving shelves for storing cups, and
elevating beds for protection from chill.

For the village, she designs tombs,
aligning doors to capture the waning sun
on winter solstice eve, measures spans
between the Stenness Stones,
does not spend much time in prayer.
She is more in obeisance to sea mists
and rain that water the grain and keep grass
green for the flocks.

LYNNE HANDY

The darkness disturbs her, the early bedtimes,
for she cannot easily sleep
going over in her mind
the work of tomorrows.

This Orcadian woman, wide-hipped,
narrow-pelvised, bears few children,
but those born of her bloodline, like me,
carry the seed of seeking.

Grandmother
--In memory of Bernice Octa Bowman

Her love was frontal, like a tank, yet she smelled of lilacs.
English heritage clung to her ungloved hands like soil
as she weeded her garden. Heeled Oxford shoes
bore her across an oaken floor to the church piano
where her strong fingers played hymns to Jesus.

Her dignity crested fierce
as the wild boar emblazoned on her family shield.
She dried her corset in the attic where no one could see,
her lady underthings as well, including slips.

A privileged girl, I curled on her blue-flocked davenport,
set on a rug of roses, cozy near the heating stove,
and watched her read the Bible, pencil in hand,
obedient to the god of her salvation.

Years passed before I understood
her god ruled a wider universe than mine.
After a tragic childhood, elopement to the wilds of Michigan,
and the death of her beloved, came her last, long widowed years,
when God sent radiation sickness, slowing her cogent mind,
stilling her busy hands, and hollowing out her bones.

King Puck

-poc: Gaelic for goat

He-goat,
denizen of rough terrain,
shaggy of coat,
scimitar-horned,
he scales the craggy Kerry hills.

Captured by Killorglin men
who bear him to a cage, raised
midtown, where he will preside,
over a trough of oats,
his whiskers in dejected pose,
his feral eyes morose,
as his jailers crowd the pubs
to celebrate the harvest home.

While crowds cheer,
a fair-haired girl in rosy frock
wreathes his tethered neck in posies,
leads him through the streets.

On the third day,
as Christ arose,
King Puck goes free
amid boisterous cries of jollity.
Up the mountainside he scrambles,
deftly dodging regicide.

Let Us Be Raucous

Lucky Puck.
In pagan times,
the he-goat's throat was slit
and he, roasted on a spit.

Ode to a Kerry Cow

She's a Kerry blue cow,
scratching
from hillside weed patches
ignored by fussier breeds
that need flowering meadows
and flowing streams to enrich
milk and cream.

It's true, she's black
but when the Irish sun
shines full
on her glossy hide,
you'd swear that she was blue.

That pail of milk!
Hosannas of fat
rise to the top,
thick and white—
just right for dolloping
on blackberries.
And Kerry butter!
Angels bless each churn
that turns cream
the color of the sun.

Best of all, the Kerry cow
and her ilk supplied milk
throughout the ages

him. I run past the machinery and when I reach the meadow, I fling out my arms and shout, "Death, you can't have my brother!"

To defeat Death, I need a sword. Near the creek, I find a stick suitable for jousting. Needing armor to cover my chest, I tear down a patch of blue morning glories, lift it over my head, and pat it in place. Then I rip part of the purple-blossomed clematis from the fence and drape it on my head.

I am invincible.

Where is my army? Troops of cattails grows alongside the creek. They'll do.

"Forward, girls!" I cry.

Marching to the house, I stand outside Finn's window and yell, "Death, you're a coward to hide beside a sick boy's bed! Come out!"

Grandma comes to the window. "Shh, Dina. You must be quiet when you play outside Finny's window."

"I am a great warrior!"

"That's nice, dear," says Grandma. "Just play quietly."

Flinging myself on the ground behind the tiger lilies, I part the leaves to spy on the window. Death surely heard me shout. Will it dare show its face? Minutes pass. Nothing happens. My troops are restless; they've grown bored lying in the grass and I tell them to hush. Then as I wait, something slithers in the tall grass beneath the window.

Death is tunneling near the house.

A blossom drops in front of my eye and I swat it away. Leaping to my feet, I shout to my army, "Follow me!"

We run past the swing set, and the forsythia bushes, and are about to dash into the lane when Death detours through the poppies. Blooms sway as if a winter wind has come rushing down from the hills. I leap into the poppy garden and beat the Orientals until they're all down; then I beat the Shirleys, the Reds, the Celadines, and the

Plumes. Finally, the poppies are all destroyed, even the white ones, and their once gorgeous heads bleed all over the ground.

"Dina!" yells Grandma, from the back porch. "Look what you did to your mother's flowers!"

Leaving my army, I run along the fencerow that parallels the asphalt road. I hear the hum of a motor and see Grandpa and Uncle Herb behind me in the pickup truck.

Grandpa calls out, "Dina, get in. It's time to say good-bye to Finny."

Grandpa stops the truck, and Uncle Herb gets out to chase me. In the middle of the meadow, he grabs me around the waist. I kick. I punch. I yell as loud as I can. I knock off his glasses. He picks them up and carries me to the truck.

Grandpa says, "Dina, why do you want to hit Uncle Herb? He's only trying to get you so you can say good-bye to Finny."

"I won't!"

"Now, is that being a nice girl?" he asks. "Poor Finny. He'll want to carry your words to heaven."

"No! No! No!"

Uncle Herb holds me firmly on his lap.

I burst into tears. "I won't tell Finn good-bye."

"Tell him whatever is in your heart," says Uncle Herb.

"That's right," says Grandpa. "Just say what you feel, honey."

By the time we reach the house, I've settled down. The preacher's gray Chevy is parked in the driveway. I'm sorry I punched and kicked Uncle Herb. I look guiltily at his glasses which now sit crookedly on his nose. In my piggy bank, there's a ten-dollar bill. I'll give it to him to buy new ones.

Grandma shakes her head. "Look at you. Dead flowers hanging from your hair."

Beth Ann's big blue eyes widen in mock wonder; then her red lips curve into a tiny, dismissive smile. She turns back to her drink.

Miranda looks uncertain. She comes from common folk and married into the city's privileged class. I hate it that she's hurt. Why are we here? I'd rather be at home with my cat. I give myself a mental pinch. We're here to get money.

I follow Miranda through the crowd. She finds our table, which is laid with white linen and set with pale orchid china and a half yard of silverware.

My cloth napkin is fashioned into a swan. I sit down, pull its tail feather, spread it across my lap, and discreetly look around. Miranda's mentor, Bunny, heiress to a south Texas ranch spanning six counties, sits directly across from me. She scowls at the empty chair on my right and sneaks looks at her diamond encrusted watch. Whoever is meant to sit there must be late.

The left end of the table is shadowed. Someone moves. A beautiful red-headed woman in a pale green dress turns toward me. Can she be Greer Garson? Garson married a Texas oil man and lives in Dallas. If the lady *is* Garson, she must be nearly ninety. Whoever she is, she's very drunk. She tips over her water glass and a waiter comes to mop up. I feel sad, remembering Garson as noble Mrs. Miniver, thwarting a wounded Nazi in her kitchen.

A large shaggy shadow passes overhead. For a moment, I think it's a bird with a large wingspan. But no, it's a man—a very tall man.

The guest Bunny was waiting for has appeared. He's around six feet eight, elderly, and wears a suit three sizes too large for his bony frame. Lowering himself into the empty chair on my right, he mutters something, which I don't catch.

"I'm sorry," I say. "I didn't hear what you said."

He turns to me. "I'm a dentist--a driller."

In the context of *driller*, *dentist* is Texan for oilman. The room is full of dentists.

His eyes take in what he can see of me—hair, face, neck, shoulders, bosom, waist, arms, hands--then he reaches a long arm across my plate toward my silverware.

His fingers maul my butter knife.

I am indignant. We lock eyes. His are pale and watery. Mine are seething.

In a soft, growly tone, he asks, "Do you know Kokopelli? Often he's depicted with a large phallus."

It isn't the pitch I'd expected. An image of Kokopelli appears in my mind: in addition to the erect phallus, he has a feathered headdress and dancing feet, and carries a bag of seeds.

Miranda has noticed his assault on my silverware. Before I can speak, she taps a warning on the back of my chair. These are *her* friends. My library is not her only charity. I mustn't cause a scene.

The driller rubs the bowl of my teaspoon. I grit my teeth.

"Perhaps you don't know who Kokopelli is," he says indulgently. "He's a Mesoamerican hump-backed fertility god, particularly venerated by southwestern Native American tribes."

I stare at my tablemates. Doesn't anyone see what this---this—*old goat* is doing? I mean, is this acceptable behavior for a member of the one percent? People turn their heads away.

The driller darts from my teaspoon to my cake fork. Moistening his lips, he fondles each tine and tells me more about Kokopelli: he's a piper and some people say his image can be seen on the full moon. The driller's long shank presses against mine under the table. I move my leg. He finds it again. I kick his ankle. He makes no sound.

I crane my neck to look at Miranda. She is gazing at the stars on the ceiling.

to Ireland's dimpled darlings,
made bold their bones,
put a shine in their eyes,
pinked their cheeks like feral posies.

Hail to the cows of Kerry,
long may they tarry
in the misted rays of the sun.
Guide their way
to heavenly pastures
when their grazing days are done.

Sacred Isle

What is that birdcall?
      I spy
a sharp-beaked magpie atop a stump,
his black eye stopped upon me.
      Whoooosh!
A sleek deer vexed by my appearance streaks
                            across the heather.
My lungs fill with mystic breath,
my fevered bones shiver.

I lie on a shamrock bed
and behold the gauzy night, sickled moon,
firefly stars, black-spanning sky.
      I dream of the sacred dead.

A copper dawn breaks.
A gentle ruff of mountains holds back the sea.
Shadows carve faces on the granite ridges.

A thousand wingflaps!
Rising up—a gulp of swallows!
Each featherbeat synchronized to keep the flock in flight.

I see life,
not just in men and beasts,
but in auras all living things release—
the grassy green that tiers up the slopes,

mists that swirl the land,
jagged hills, pouting skies.

Cut high
with harvest scythes.
What else is truth?
Tend the crops. Kill an ox
to keep gods happy.
Kiss the fish and let him go.

The Ferry Fly

On the *Dublin Swift*,
I bounce into a comfy chair
in the upper lounge,
near a bar serving tea and wine,
and settle in for a two-hour ride
next a window
framing the rolling sea.

Each undulation I honor—
my breath silvers
like sun-glints on the waves.
A holy consecration
grips my imagination.
I am a speck
rocked in a great watery cradle.
Irish Sea, I feel your pulse!
Conveyor of saints,
heal my flagging faith!

Then a ferry fly begins a window-crawl.
Small and desperate, he beats his wings
against the glassy pane,
wanting sky.

I try to cup him in my hand
and take him out on deck,
but with a frisson of wings,

Let Us Be Raucous

he darts away.
Why is he blind to the exit doors?

Sea angels,
give me a gentler truth—
something I can bear—than a fly
snared in a world of his own making.

Gathering the Mistletoe

--After The Druids—Bringing in the Mistletoe,
painted by George Henry and E. A. Hornel, 1890

One slash of the golden sickle--
the Celtic chieftain aborts the mistletoe,
rooted in the oak like a nesting fetus.
Majestically, he climbs down, drapes
green garlands over the heads
of two bone-white bulls,
apportions some to priests,
and in crimson robe,
heads the procession downhill
to the sacred stones.

The winter moon creeps over the crest,
partially concealed by spirit waftings.
An oratorio breeze weaves
the message of hunger
with pleas for plenty come spring.
With open maws and eyes,
ancient oaks chant old spells.
Druids, faces the color of old roots,
tread softly
on long-toed feet through dewy gorse.
Mists rise, shadowing man as he lifts himself
to insane heights,
seeking to appease perfidious gods.

The bulls will not make the journey back.

Short Stories

Dina, Warrior Child

My brother, who is two years older than me, has a tumor with tentacles that are choking his brain. In a dark corner of Finn's room, Death waits. People speak in low voices. They walk softly; their bodies sag. I sit in an alcove trying to read but can't concentrate because my mind is wild. Throwing down the book, I stomp from the house making loud growling noises, wanting Death to fear me. I run past the garden filled with dazzling poppies: purple, orange, crimson, peach, and white. It's the white ones whose egg-shaped pods contain the milk that helps Finn sleep. Sometimes he hurts so much he thrashes and breaks the spindles on his headboard.

When the poppy leaves wither, Mommy slits the pods, collects the sap, and boils it in water and lime. It smells musky, like dirty socks. Scum settles on the top. Using a spoon, she lifts it to dry, and then adds the powder to Finn's apple juice and gives it to him.

Only Daddy and I know what Mommy does with the white poppies.

The tractor is parked in the barn lot, still hitched to the harrow. Daddy is in the east field when Mommy sends Uncle Herb to fetch

She starts to remove them, but Uncle Herb says, "She's fine, Ma. Leave the flowers alone."

Mommy and Daddy are in Finn's room. The preacher sits beside the bed. He offers his chair to me. I sit down and look at my brother's face. Mommy must have given him some of her medicine because he lies unmoving with closed eyes. I find his icy hand and rub it to give him warmth. I am swollen with feelings and don't know what to say. Then his chest inflates; he exhales and I arch over him to catch his breath in my mouth. Closing my lips, I hold it there, feel it seep into my lungs and spread through my body.

I become Finn.

"He's gone," says the preacher.

He begins saying the Twenty-Third Psalm. Mommy cries. My grandparents and uncle come into the room. I go to the alcove and sit, feeling my brother settle in my soul.

Published in *Lark's Fiction Magazine*, Issue 15, September, 2012

Walls

My room is wallpapered in tea roses. Lining both window sills is a collection of ceramic flowers, all pink. Pink is a gentle color, and I need it around me because farm life isn't always gentle. Cattle and hogs groan when they're hit with stock prods to herd them onto my father's truck bound for the stockyards and they scream at the sight of the sledgehammer, when they're killed for butchering. Young bulls set up a howl when they're castrated. Sheep bleat when they're shorn. Chickens squawk when they see Mother with her .22 rifle. A crack shot, she shoots them through their heads. I seek protection from things that happen in the barnyard. It helps that my room is on the east side of the house, and all that killing and maiming and shearing happens on the west side.

It's 1953. I'm thirteen and pudgy, and secretly fear I'll end up fat like my mother. One of my father's acquaintances calls me a "rosy-cheeked farm girl," and I find the image so unflattering that I resolve to make myself thin. After discussing the matter with Mother, who is busy with one of her crafts, I begin a diet of orange soda pop and cheese sandwiches. By springtime, I weigh 110 pounds and measure 32-22-32.

Boys notice me, but I'm more interested in Daphne DuMaurier novels, my church youth group, cheerleading, and writing poems. Mother never discusses sex with me. She doesn't even call things by their right names: urinating is "tinkling," defecating is "tinkling big," a boy's penis is a "sprinkler," and the orifices on a female between her tailbone and pubic bone are bundled into one word, "bucket." A fart is a "bucket sneeze."

Menstrual periods are burdens for a young girl who likes to turn cartwheels. My first period starts at school and despite hearing about menstruation in health class, I am genuinely startled when I find blood stains on the crotch of my underpants. I don't know who to ask for a sanitary napkin, so I fold several sheets of toilet paper together and stuff them in the crotch of my underpants. As long as the flow is light, the toilet paper works, but when it becomes heavy, I'm forced to tell Mother, who fits me with a sanitary belt and gives me a box of napkins. After several months of dieting, my period stops altogether and I don't give it much thought.

Eventually I tell Mother.

That is my undoing.

"I'm not having periods anymore," I say.

Mother looks up from pouring acid on a metal tray. "How many have you missed?"

"I don't know. Maybe two or three."

She doesn't say anything, but a tiny frown dimples her brow. I go to my bedroom and sit on a hassock Mother has created from three taped-together tomato juice cans, padded, and upholstered in pink gingham. I memorize the Beatitudes. Next Sunday, the youth group holds the service and since I'm the president, I have to give the sermon.

Two mornings later, when I enter the kitchen for breakfast, Mother says, "We're going to town this morning."

I yawn, not quite awake. "It's a school day."

"I'll take you to school afterward," says Mother. "Be sure to wear a skirt."

Now I'm alert. "Why?"

She doesn't respond, and I see from the set of her jaw that she's not going to explain. After drinking a glass of water and eating a slice of cheese, I go to my room, put on a blue skirt and blouse, and slip my feet into white socks and a pair of white buck loafers.

Mother is up to something. Uneasily, I climb into her gray Chevrolet. Once we head down the road, she reveals that we're going to see Dr. Yurley, the physician who delivered my younger siblings and me.

"Why?" I ask.

Mother brakes at a stop sign and doesn't answer. The news that I'm going to see Dr. Yurley puts me in a bad mood because I don't like him. He's a sullen man, who smells of cigars and clears his throat in loud wet growls. He's also given me shots.

We travel the ten miles to town on an asphalt road flanked by stubbly fields and Mother parks in front of the doctor's office. The waiting room is empty and the receptionist shows us into the examining room, which has poison green walls and smells of disinfectant. A cowhide armchair sets near the window. The doctor's desk is littered with thick books lying on their spines, split down the middle like slaughtered doves.

In the middle of the room is the leather-topped examining table, which I remember well from my tonsillectomy four years earlier.

Dr. Yurley stands beside the examining table. He's a hulk. His pores are extra-large and you can see each hair of his bushy eyebrows and mustache growing out of his skin. Each hair has its own tiny ring of dandruff. He has a prominent nose, shrewd piggy eyes, and jowls.

He and Mother exchange glances. Avoiding eye contact with me, Mother sits in the chair and puts her purse on her lap.

"Take off your underpants," she says briskly.

"Why?" I yell.

"Take them off."

I sob bitterly, but slip off my underpants and grip them in both hands.

"Get up on the examining table," says Mother.

"I don't want to!"

"Do as I say," she commands, using her "tough" voice.

I step on a little stool and lift myself onto the table.

"Open your legs," says Dr. Yurley, pulling out two metal loops. "I want you to put your feet in these stirrups."

I won't do it! I cross my ankles. Mother threatens to spank.

"Help me, Jesus!" I cry.

"Oh, for heaven's sake," says Mother.

I hope Jesus will strike Dr. Yurley dead, but he doesn't. Nothing deters the doctor from prying my ankles apart, thrusting my feet in the stirrups, flipping up my skirt and sticking his hand—I'm sure it's his whole hand—inside me. I cry out because he's hurting me.

Then I catch a look in his eyes. Is it pleasure? Is it triumph? Does he like feeling inside me. Does he enjoy tormenting helpless young girls? Is this rape? Why would Mother let him rape me? I try to escape by lunging toward the edge of the table but the doctor grabs me and puts an iron hand on my stomach.

"Lie still," orders Mother.

It dawns on me that Mother thinks I'm pregnant.

How could she think I'd had intercourse? I've never even kissed a boy.

With a jolt, I remember the veterinarian who recently visited the farm; he stuck his arm in the pelvis of a bawling heifer.

That's me: no better than a cow.

"I AM NOT LIVESTOCK!" I yell.

Mother finally looks at me. "Of course, you're not," she says curtly.

Dr. Yurley withdraws his hand and pulls down my skirt. I climb down from the table and pull on my underpants. My female parts feel raw. I keep my head low, feeling shamed. Mother tells me to go to the waiting room.

There are others in the room now. A farmer. The school superintendent's wife. A woman with a baby. They stare at me. Above the fireplace is a print of a Victorian doctor standing beside the sickbed of a small child. I look at it carefully; the doctor looks kind and gentle and thoughtful. I wonder if Dr. Yurley sees himself that way.

Soon Mother emerges from the office, and we get in the car and drive away. Neither of us speaks. I hate her. I press my body against the car door so hard that the armrest cuts into my rib cage.

She drops me off at school. I go to the restroom and sit inside a cubicle and weep. Until today, I'd never thought much about my sex; it was an unused part of me, something personal to be dealt with when I became an adult. Now, I feel debased and humiliated.

I've lost the comfort zone that was my innocence and I've learned two hard lessons: I can't count on Mother and I can't count on Jesus.

That night I bathe in the family tub, the tub that also held water to cleanse the bodies of my father, mother, and two little sisters, and before that, my maternal grandparents, and maybe before that, my great-grandmother. I lather myself well. After my bath, I dry myself on a white towel, stiff from the clothesline. It feels like I imagine sackcloth feels. Putting on my robe, I open the door. Mother sits at the kitchen table reading an Ellery Queen mystery, and I have to walk past her to reach my bedroom.

"Do you have anything to tell me?" Mother asks coldly.

"No," I mutter.

Mother asks the question every night for a week and then stops. I begin eating normally; maintain my weight and my menses flow again.

She and I never speak of the visit to Dr. Yurley, but the memory stains me, and I erect walls between myself and everyone who comes into my life.

Who can you trust, if you can't trust Mother or Jesus?

Me Too

Miranda and I enter a ballroom set up for the annual library fundraiser. Twinkling globes, undulating gold and silver streamers, and glittering stars pasted on the ceiling meet our eyes. A baritone in a milky-blue suit sings a Willie Nelson tune. Conversation patters; often there's a burst of laughter.

The city's elite are here. Bouffant-haired women tighten their spines in designer dresses. Broad-chested men, some with flab rolling over their belts, sport western-cut jackets with sequined lapels.

As the new director of a regional library system in need of funds, I've come to the gala at the behest of Miranda, my board chair, to solicit money for literacy programs. I'd rather apply for grants because I don't schmooze well, but here I am, dressed in an understated navy-blue dress and rope of faux pearls.

Miranda introduces me to Beth Ann, my congresswoman. An attractive blonde in a white pantsuit, Beth Ann licks salt off her margarita rim and says hello. I offer my hand, knowing she belongs to the political party that consistently cuts library funding.

"It's so good to see you, Beth Ann," gushes Miranda. "I hope you're well."

"Doing fine," says the congresswoman. "How was Kenya?"

"Barker and I had a marvelous trip," responds Miranda. "We saw the white rhinos."

"Kokopelli is more like Pan, the great reveler," the driller whispers.

With lightning speed, he lunges across my upper torso and passionately strokes my dinner fork. "He's quite a fellow," he pants. "Carries newborns in his hump, along with the seeds. When women hear his flute, they flee to the desert."

I shove my chair away from the table. He yanks it back, nudging my right breast, and then reaches for my dinner knife. He rubs it feverishly.

His eyelashes flutter.

"Kokopelli rapes, but women enjoy it," he says. "He pleasures them, you know."

Then he leans back in his chair and takes a deep breath. Except for my soup spoon, he has violated every utensil in my place setting.

Miranda, Bunny, Greer, and the others at the table seem to be ignoring the driller and me. They speak to each other in sparkling dabs of conversation. "How was Antarctica?" "We found Borneo divine." "Algiers is nothing without the Casbah."

Bunny has been watching though, for at this point, Miranda leans behind me and hisses a warning: Bunny is playing matchmaker for Greer and the driller, and he's paying too much attention to me.

By now I am fit to be tied. I look at the driller. He is staring at my pristine, unsullied soup spoon. What he does next will determine whether I leave the table and call a cab.

I wait.

His indifference washes over me like a blessing. He turns to face his peers. "Last year," he says in an imperious tone, "I hunted tigers in Tanzania."

"Truly?" replies Bunny's husband. "In November, Bunny and I went to Cambodia to see the Irrawaddy dolphins."

"Barker and I vacationed in Kenya," offers Miranda. "On safari, you know."

Now the band plays "Smoke Gets in Your Eyes." A streamer breaks free and floats down, draping the driller's shoulders in gold: all he needs is a scepter. A server comes with the soup, a mushroom consommé with a wonderful aroma, and sets my bowl in front of me. I take a sip with my undefiled spoon and clean the rest of my silverware with a sanitizing towelette I carry in my purse.

On my way home, I realize I was so distracted by the driller that I forgot to ask anyone for funds for my literacy programs. I'm glad to be free of the rarified ambience of the very rich. I'm glad to be me with my tiny apartment, four-year-old car, crochety cat, and no immediate plans to visit exotic places. Before I unlock my door, I look up at the moon.

I wish I had remembered to tell the driller that the face on the moon is a woman's--no crook-backed god with erect member to fire the savage fantasies of dry old men, but a lovely woman whom Aeschylus, the Greek playwright, called the "eye of night," controller of tides, menses, diaries, and destinies. Most importantly, her mind is on the universe.

www.ingramcontent.com/pod-product-compliance
Lightning Source LLC
Chambersburg PA
CBHW060817050426
42449CB00008B/1696